MONTHLY BILL
PAYING ORGANIZER

SPEEDY PUBLISHING

Speedy Publishing LLC
40 E. Main St. #1156
Newark, DE 19711

www.SpeedyPublishing.Com

Copyright 2014

MONTH: **DATE:**

BILLS	AMOUNT	DUE ON	PAID

BILL TRACKING

MONTH:

BILL	AMOUNT
Mortgage	
Water	
Electricity	
Internet	
Cable	
Cell Phones	
Loan	
Insurance	
Others	
TOTAL	

MONTH:

BILL	AMOUNT
Mortgage	
Water	
Electricity	
Internet	
Cable	
Cell Phones	
Loan	
Insurance	
Others	
TOTAL	

MONTH:

BILL	AMOUNT
Mortgage	
Water	
Electricity	
Internet	
Cable	
Cell Phones	
Loan	
Insurance	
Others	
TOTAL	

MONTH:

BILL	AMOUNT
Mortgage	
Water	
Electricity	
Internet	
Cable	
Cell Phones	
Loan	
Insurance	
Others	
TOTAL	

NOTES

REMINDERS

EXPENSES

BUDGET

MONTH: DATE:

BILLS	AMOUNT	DUE ON	PAID
BILLS	AMOUNT	DUE ON	PAID

BILL TRACKING

MONTH:

BILL	AMOUNT
Mortgage	
Water	
Electricity	
Internet	
Cable	
Cell Phones	
Loan	
Insurance	
Others	
TOTAL	

MONTH:

BILL	AMOUNT
Mortgage	
Water	
Electricity	
Internet	
Cable	
Cell Phones	
Loan	
Insurance	
Others	
TOTAL	

MONTH:

BILL	AMOUNT
Mortgage	
Water	
Electricity	
Internet	
Cable	
Cell Phones	
Loan	
Insurance	
Others	
TOTAL	

MONTH:

BILL	AMOUNT
Mortgage	
Water	
Electricity	
Internet	
Cable	
Cell Phones	
Loan	
Insurance	
Others	
TOTAL	

NOTES

REMINDERS

EXPENSES

BUDGET

MONTH: DATE:

BILLS	AMOUNT	DUE ON	PAID

BILL TRACKING

MONTH: **MONTH:**

BILL	AMOUNT	BILL	AMOUNT
Mortgage		Mortgage	
Water		Water	
Electricity		Electricity	
Internet		Internet	
Cable		Cable	
Cell Phones		Cell Phones	
Loan		Loan	
Insurance		Insurance	
Others		Others	
TOTAL		**TOTAL**	

MONTH: **MONTH:**

BILL	AMOUNT	BILL	AMOUNT
Mortgage		Mortgage	
Water		Water	
Electricity		Electricity	
Internet		Internet	
Cable		Cable	
Cell Phones		Cell Phones	
Loan		Loan	
Insurance		Insurance	
Others		Others	
TOTAL		**TOTAL**	

NOTES

REMINDERS

EXPENSES

BUDGET

MONTH: DATE:

BILLS	AMOUNT	DUE ON	PAID

BILL TRACKING

MONTH:

BILL	AMOUNT	BILL	AMOUNT
Mortgage		Mortgage	
Water		Water	
Electricity		Electricity	
Internet		Internet	
Cable		Cable	
Cell Phones		Cell Phones	
Loan		Loan	
Insurance		Insurance	
Others		Others	
TOTAL		**TOTAL**	

MONTH:

BILL	AMOUNT	BILL	AMOUNT
Mortgage		Mortgage	
Water		Water	
Electricity		Electricity	
Internet		Internet	
Cable		Cable	
Cell Phones		Cell Phones	
Loan		Loan	
Insurance		Insurance	
Others		Others	
TOTAL		**TOTAL**	

NOTES

REMINDERS

EXPENSES

BUDGET

MONTH: DATE:

BILLS	AMOUNT	DUE ON	PAID

BILL TRACKING

MONTH:

BILL	AMOUNT	BILL	AMOUNT
Mortgage		Mortgage	
Water		Water	
Electricity		Electricity	
Internet		Internet	
Cable		Cable	
Cell Phones		Cell Phones	
Loan		Loan	
Insurance		Insurance	
Others		Others	
TOTAL		**TOTAL**	

MONTH:

BILL	AMOUNT	BILL	AMOUNT
Mortgage		Mortgage	
Water		Water	
Electricity		Electricity	
Internet		Internet	
Cable		Cable	
Cell Phones		Cell Phones	
Loan		Loan	
Insurance		Insurance	
Others		Others	
TOTAL		**TOTAL**	

<table>
<tr><td>NOTES</td><td>REMINDERS</td></tr>
<tr><td>EXPENSES</td><td>BUDGET</td></tr>
</table>

MONTH: DATE:

BILLS	AMOUNT	DUE ON	PAID

BILL TRACKING

MONTH: **MONTH:**

BILL	AMOUNT	BILL	AMOUNT
Mortgage		Mortgage	
Water		Water	
Electricity		Electricity	
Internet		Internet	
Cable		Cable	
Cell Phones		Cell Phones	
Loan		Loan	
Insurance		Insurance	
Others		Others	
TOTAL		**TOTAL**	

MONTH: **MONTH:**

BILL	AMOUNT	BILL	AMOUNT
Mortgage		Mortgage	
Water		Water	
Electricity		Electricity	
Internet		Internet	
Cable		Cable	
Cell Phones		Cell Phones	
Loan		Loan	
Insurance		Insurance	
Others		Others	
TOTAL		**TOTAL**	

NOTES
REMINDERS
EXPENSES
BUDGET

MONTH:　　　　　　　　　　**DATE:**

BILLS	AMOUNT	DUE ON	PAID

BILL TRACKING

MONTH:

BILL	AMOUNT
Mortgage	
Water	
Electricity	
Internet	
Cable	
Cell Phones	
Loan	
Insurance	
Others	
TOTAL	

MONTH:

BILL	AMOUNT
Mortgage	
Water	
Electricity	
Internet	
Cable	
Cell Phones	
Loan	
Insurance	
Others	
TOTAL	

MONTH:

BILL	AMOUNT
Mortgage	
Water	
Electricity	
Internet	
Cable	
Cell Phones	
Loan	
Insurance	
Others	
TOTAL	

MONTH:

BILL	AMOUNT
Mortgage	
Water	
Electricity	
Internet	
Cable	
Cell Phones	
Loan	
Insurance	
Others	
TOTAL	

NOTES

REMINDERS

EXPENSES

BUDGET

MONTH: DATE:

BILLS	AMOUNT	DUE ON	PAID
BILLS	AMOUNT	DUE ON	PAID

BILL TRACKING

MONTH: _______

BILL	AMOUNT
Mortgage	
Water	
Electricity	
Internet	
Cable	
Cell Phones	
Loan	
Insurance	
Others	
TOTAL	

MONTH: _______

BILL	AMOUNT
Mortgage	
Water	
Electricity	
Internet	
Cable	
Cell Phones	
Loan	
Insurance	
Others	
TOTAL	

MONTH: _______

BILL	AMOUNT
Mortgage	
Water	
Electricity	
Internet	
Cable	
Cell Phones	
Loan	
Insurance	
Others	
TOTAL	

MONTH: _______

BILL	AMOUNT
Mortgage	
Water	
Electricity	
Internet	
Cable	
Cell Phones	
Loan	
Insurance	
Others	
TOTAL	

NOTES

REMINDERS

EXPENSES

BUDGET

MONTH: DATE:

BILLS	AMOUNT	DUE ON	PAID

BILL TRACKING

MONTH:

BILL	AMOUNT	BILL	AMOUNT
Mortgage		Mortgage	
Water		Water	
Electricity		Electricity	
Internet		Internet	
Cable		Cable	
Cell Phones		Cell Phones	
Loan		Loan	
Insurance		Insurance	
Others		Others	
TOTAL		**TOTAL**	

MONTH:

BILL	AMOUNT	BILL	AMOUNT
Mortgage		Mortgage	
Water		Water	
Electricity		Electricity	
Internet		Internet	
Cable		Cable	
Cell Phones		Cell Phones	
Loan		Loan	
Insurance		Insurance	
Others		Others	
TOTAL		**TOTAL**	

<table>
<tr><td>NOTES</td><td>REMINDERS</td></tr>
<tr><td>EXPENSES</td><td>BUDGET</td></tr>
</table>

MONTH: DATE:

BILLS	AMOUNT	DUE ON	PAID

BILL TRACKING

MONTH: **MONTH:**

BILL	AMOUNT	BILL	AMOUNT
Mortgage		Mortgage	
Water		Water	
Electricity		Electricity	
Internet		Internet	
Cable		Cable	
Cell Phones		Cell Phones	
Loan		Loan	
Insurance		Insurance	
Others		Others	
TOTAL		**TOTAL**	

MONTH: **MONTH:**

BILL	AMOUNT	BILL	AMOUNT
Mortgage		Mortgage	
Water		Water	
Electricity		Electricity	
Internet		Internet	
Cable		Cable	
Cell Phones		Cell Phones	
Loan		Loan	
Insurance		Insurance	
Others		Others	
TOTAL		**TOTAL**	

NOTES

REMINDERS

EXPENSES

BUDGET

MONTH: DATE:

BILLS	AMOUNT	DUE ON	PAID

BILL TRACKING

MONTH:

BILL	AMOUNT	BILL	AMOUNT
Mortgage		Mortgage	
Water		Water	
Electricity		Electricity	
Internet		Internet	
Cable		Cable	
Cell Phones		Cell Phones	
Loan		Loan	
Insurance		Insurance	
Others		Others	
TOTAL		**TOTAL**	

MONTH:

BILL	AMOUNT	BILL	AMOUNT
Mortgage		Mortgage	
Water		Water	
Electricity		Electricity	
Internet		Internet	
Cable		Cable	
Cell Phones		Cell Phones	
Loan		Loan	
Insurance		Insurance	
Others		Others	
TOTAL		**TOTAL**	

NOTES

REMINDERS

EXPENSES

BUDGET

BILLS	AMOUNT	DUE ON	PAID
BILLS	AMOUNT	DUE ON	PAID

BILL TRACKING

MONTH:

BILL	AMOUNT
Mortgage	
Water	
Electricity	
Internet	
Cable	
Cell Phones	
Loan	
Insurance	
Others	
TOTAL	

MONTH:

BILL	AMOUNT
Mortgage	
Water	
Electricity	
Internet	
Cable	
Cell Phones	
Loan	
Insurance	
Others	
TOTAL	

MONTH:

BILL	AMOUNT
Mortgage	
Water	
Electricity	
Internet	
Cable	
Cell Phones	
Loan	
Insurance	
Others	
TOTAL	

MONTH:

BILL	AMOUNT
Mortgage	
Water	
Electricity	
Internet	
Cable	
Cell Phones	
Loan	
Insurance	
Others	
TOTAL	

<table>
<tr><td>NOTES</td><td>REMINDERS</td></tr>
<tr><td>EXPENSES</td><td>BUDGET</td></tr>
</table>

MONTH: DATE:

BILLS	AMOUNT	DUE ON	PAID

BILL TRACKING

MONTH: _______________   **MONTH:** _______________

BILL	AMOUNT	BILL	AMOUNT
Mortgage		Mortgage	
Water		Water	
Electricity		Electricity	
Internet		Internet	
Cable		Cable	
Cell Phones		Cell Phones	
Loan		Loan	
Insurance		Insurance	
Others		Others	
TOTAL		**TOTAL**	

MONTH: _______________   **MONTH:** _______________

BILL	AMOUNT	BILL	AMOUNT
Mortgage		Mortgage	
Water		Water	
Electricity		Electricity	
Internet		Internet	
Cable		Cable	
Cell Phones		Cell Phones	
Loan		Loan	
Insurance		Insurance	
Others		Others	
TOTAL		**TOTAL**	

NOTES	REMINDERS

EXPENSES	BUDGET